Beyond

© Rosemary Gallaher, 2019
All rights reserved.

Out There

Beyond the Fringe

You've got a house on the edge of town
where the smog disappears and leaves bright, scattered stars
and the night tastes as cold as winters on Mars
and nobody ever comes 'round.

City folk say that there's nothing to see
but I've been to the borders, I take off my shoes
and I cross russet fields where the fences are loose
near your shack and I almost feel free.

I will knock on your door one day soon
and I won't be afraid, as they say I should be
but I'll ask if there's anything out there, if you've seen
a world beyond our own.

I want to know your velvet skies.
In the schools they don't teach us to love, to explore.
My days are barbed wire; my nights feel like *more*.
Captivate me and open my eyes.

Far from the industrial din
I wonder if I would hear the beat of my heart
intertwining with yours like a duet part
  nd if the stars would hear us sing.

Take my hand when I arrive.

The cold is different where you are; it's getting warm
so let's cross the boundaries, go into the storm
where even the air feels alive.

Whisper

Eyes solemn as pinewood
The touch of your hand
The river's at half-tide
They don't understand
The night is still falling
Don't know you like me
When sun breaks the morning
By sunlight you'll see
We whispered 'mongst spring-blooms
A promise to keep
When we were both yearlings
The valley is steep
My hands through your mane now
As sure as the day
Fly free as the meadows
Where grass finches play
Our eyes are still keen and
Our hearts don't know grey
With these limbs like greenlings
I'll take you away.

Anatomy of a Distant Star

You are made of stardust,
a universe condensed into one human body
and it's no wonder that sometimes you dream of escape.

You tell me that you're restless,
itching to get back to your home in the living sky
and that your heart is turbulence,
your centre is molten core.

You and I, at this second,
are a burst of summer, a shivering grass-stalk,
the first treble note in a starlet's cry.
We are only a fraction of what we were and will be.

Paradise

This morning the city slid past me.

My train travelled on while the world as I knew it

just slipped out of view.

My destination was the sweetest paradise;

my intent: to bring it home to you.

And when I reached it

they told me that I could take back nothing but a poem.

I despaired

because I knew that simple words would never do.

In Another Tongue, In a Far-Off Town

Sometimes I dream that we met in a place

where sadness was a foreign language

where you couldn't understand the words I whispered in your ear.

Where I couldn't taste it like molasses on your tongue or read it in

your smudging script,

see it painted on your face or feel it, warm between your thighs.

Sometimes I dream that I met you in some other fashion,

stumbling over unfamiliar lines

but not here. Not here.

Chance Meetings

We didn't meet in a wild rain. We met in a corridor
with bandaids on our arms from the blood tests
but you made me feel torrential,
like beyond all of this or inside all of this
we're still young and burning and free.

We don't feel sad anymore.
Sadness is just the tip of the iceberg, a thin mist that covers our everything.
All moments are sad but so many thoughts and feelings swirl within that sadness,
a complexity of love and of laughter and happiness, even.

Time might be short but our hearts are expansive.
I am a vast ocean. With a tip of your head you're my travel plan;
holding tickets to a future that I didn't think I'd find here
you're the nightlife in London and breakfast in France.

We didn't meet under starlight but like a stranger on the street corner
I knew that I would find you
wrapped up in me when it's too cold to sleep
and our chances too bleak to go home.
We didn't meet in a nightclub but it's *loud*, how much I love you.
I don't care if I never see you in the rain.

Can You Hear Them?

Our lips crash and
cannons roar.
Outside this four-walled sanctuary our ancestors wage unholy war
but they don't know violence,
real violence.

It's not the flames rising high above their corpses,
it's not a spinning coin;

It's the way your fevered hands grip my skin,
it's the motion, fast-paced and desperate, a dance,
it's the ricocheting colours that skirt my vision when you smile,

The laughter wrenched from my throat when you whisper a joke

And the gaping black abyss,
a sick, accursed rift,
All that is left when you leave.

Where Water Turns to Air

Rain spotlights the silver in those eyes.

Amidst the drumming, against the backdrop of the distant drone, a pleasant surprise.

Boy with raven's hair; higher than the dragon's wings,
we dine like kings,
for once the water's surface too ethereal, too tempting
not to dip in.

Snow

Let's lose our faces tonight,
chemical anxiety and paper highs
thrown to the curb by something stronger, small and white
while stars burn out their insides; Prometheus in the sky.

I always thought you were a lie:
stinking pop culture curling bright around my eye
but now I wonder if your treasure is something I could find,
leaping from the bass lines into my frenzied, eager mind.

Feathers

The sky became hers to explore.

Flyaway

Little tragedies fall on the streets

like raffle tickets that somebody needs

But drops before the lot is drawn,

lost in the gutters, damp and torn.

Little victories lift them away

like a cool breeze on a summer day,

announcing new life at the break of dawn,

Carried away by a silver morn.

And where do all these stories go?

Out through the back roads where nobody knows.

See them and touch them but don't follow,

they're already gone.

Sublime

Out there:

where the words flow freely

and the nomad rediscovers herself,

where sunburnt hills and secret gullies tell ancient histories

of *we are together*,

I kneel at the alter of a million maps

pointing towards the sublime, the sacred, the truth of it all

and I sing

like a thrumming heartbeat

out there, out there, out there, out there, out there.

Dark and Light

Malaise

You were painful
like dry-swallowing pills on an empty stomach;
like blasting music loudly enough to forget my name.
But I was young, and I believed you
when you said that beauty was pain.

As Obvious as Neon Signs

Last night I picked you up from a glass-littered street corner
and helped you wipe bile from your strands of flaxen hair.
You sang under your breath as you stumbled into the car.
I turned corners while streetlights shimmered in the drops on the windscreen
and you fell asleep trying to tell me that you used to know better than this.
It's not that I mind
(I'd spend every night combing seedy cities if it meant keeping you safe)
but
your eyes haven't smiled in a year now
and I wish that I knew what it would take to make you happy
because between cheap liquor, cold nights and bad lovers
I haven't got a clue.

I'm Sorry that You're Worried

I don't know how I turned into
a girl made of scrap paper.
It's strange that we're both liars now;
you know but never ask.
I wish I could be a sonnet for you,
a new-smelling book or a painting for you.
I don't know what *healthy* is anymore,
but I know it isn't this.

Inanity

When feel-good films were mentioned in my English class, the
teacher used to utter the word platitudes as if it had a sour taste
as if there was something wrong with making people happy,
as if a smile wasn't worth the twelve-or-so muscles it took to put it
there.

Some people glamorise darkness, and I wonder if they've ever
touched the real kind –
the one that's ice-cold,
uncompromising,
the one that shakes you day in and day out until you're every
definition of exhausted
and you've still got to keep pushing
on.

I don't think they'd want it if they knew.

When I was five I believed that there was something different
about me; some tick in the mechanics and I think I'm relearning
that now.

I just want happiness, no matter how cheaply it comes or how
briefly it stays
happiness like a trip to the gas station or an unexpected
compliment;
happiness like a sprint through the rain.

Maybe I'm a succubus, wild for it,

maybe I'm an innocent girl.

I'm a child who tells everyone that I've got it already; I want it that badly,

and I parade it around like my best Sunday dress

hoping everyone thinks that it's mine.

Normality

Everything closes off after a while. In therapy it's likened to a *shrinking world*.

Options get fewer and plans become unrealistic. It's still okay. It's still okay.

Normal is raw skin, 4am showers; thoughts that seep like carcinogens into your dreams.

Last Sunday a man kissed your cheek when you gave him your (fake) number. You smiled and went home and scrubbed your face for twenty minutes. He didn't know.

You're always trying. There's nothing else to do, really, but try. And sometimes you'll skip meals because meals aren't clean or wash your hands a few more times than the doctor recommended but that's alright because the next day you'll touch something you've been avoiding and feel like a queen, and
normal might never be travelling, loud parties or children when you're middle-aged.
But that's okay. You're learning it's okay.

December 21st

Hands held tight
while the earth takes flight,
steep plunge and scarring red,
molten screams,
lucid dream,
choking flames and acid sky,
clouded by salt tears,
last loving smile
before the abyss eats us whole.

No.

Champagne laughter, whirlwind music, collective happy sigh,
stoke the embers,
mark the year
and breathing starts again.

But sometimes
I wish the world would end.

Bloom

It's normal, you know.

Bruises flower under skin like lilies in a garden,

tears find their place just like water in the soil.

They seep into the black,

nurture seedlings

and hurt grows so green and natural.

Pearl skin is *supposed* to go purple,

It's as right as the rain.

So don't worry, don't fret,

I'm art, you know, cross-stitching on the wall,

an ivory piano key

just as I should be

because battered things are beautiful.

Feathers torn from silk pillows

and stick figures on balance beams

.Aren't as loved, nor as adored,

nor as beautiful as me.

Escape Route

Rose-hued sand desert,

I'm lying here waiting,

black birds overhead

and my long unkempt hair.

Where did this come from?

The helpless frustrating

do-nothing-ness while

they attack without care?

And how did I get here?

And why do I wander

through sick mirage sand-dunes

so bright but alone?

And where's my escape route?

And how do I find her?

A car on some highway

to take me back home.

Mining for Emeralds

Those green eyes always skirt the edge of cataclysm
dancing in circles 'round a bonfire self-destruction.
Closer,
closer,
see how close I can get to the ledge?

Trapping sand and throwing bottles into the flames,
smashed glass,
littered pieces,
more sand to run through your fingers,
gaze beseeching.
Look what I can do.

Breathing in the fire's hiss
your mind draws back as you lean in for the kiss,
ensnared like an animal,
Trapped in the cycle,
blood on your palms and vodka misting your breath,
the only tears you know how to spill.

River Dog Part 1

Mum and Dad said they sent you to
live on a farm and I
know what that means
and I
know just what happens
to creatures like you.

I wonder if those first weeks
would have made any difference
if we'd taught you to
sit, stay,
the right things to do.

It's been years and my siblings
are riling for a new you.
I wonder if they know you;
know your fate
like I do.

I was never a child,
not like them
nor like you.

I don't want you,
I fear you,
but I miss you and miss you

and I've wondered if I could be
wild like you.

But my innocence died on a table
with you.

River Dog Part 2

Black fur on the prairie,

Hope where I thought there wasn't any,

Lies that children tell blown away like smoke above the river ferry.

Lick my hand like candy,

Ice cream days and miscellany,

Hugs before we go back to the city, see you later, bush fairy.

Reasons to Stay

You're like guitar chords by the creek on the first day of summer,
like brightly-coloured bags in the back of the car,
like lanterns and board-games and friends' birthday parties,
new stories but the same places every year.
You're like glimpses of futures, like wild possibilities,
I'm chasing your strings down old streets with fresh eyes,
because you're like colours on canvas, a whirlwind, yet balanced,
somewhere I left a lottery ticket for a love of this kind.
You're like sing-alongs on Sundays and a normal happy life,
you're like ties in the mornings and pancakes and life,
you're like freesias in gardens and life, life, life, life,
and god, I want to care about life.

Water Pressure

My limbs shake and it's all *heavy heavy heavy* –
somewhere, the surface molecules want me to rise.
Lungs like burning stars are my only hope now,
fractured light in the water is my only guide.

Above the deep blue, a bright, beckoning spectrum
of colour and life beams as clearly as day.
Let this darkness dissipate and let sunlight take its place.
Move oceans and let sadness fall away.

If Every Second was a Perfect Sound

I realised yesterday
that there is no time in life for half-measures.
When I love people I want to love them loudly enough that they know it.
I want to tie my heart to the sleeves of every passer-by,
so that they understand how much I want them around.
I want to write love on scrap paper and tuck it into the crevices in walls like a birthday wish,
and never let misanthropy grow where it shouldn't be.
The sun burns itself just to send light out for thousands of miles and keep us alive.
I want to try.

Good Morning, Dreams are Calling

We sing about infinity
from the back of a moving bus,
because the mountains have heard our names a thousand times.
We are the sunlight rays bending into hues of vermilion and rose,
we are the bursts of air beneath a hummingbird's wings
and in the expanse of space, our fears become small.

Arrival

Autumn leaves, tartan cases
and me on the late train –
birds sing in high places
as I finally arrive.
The breath of relief now
becomes a smooth, steady rhythm
flowing into something greater;
something fresh and alive.
I crawled beneath track lines
with metal clutching my fingers
to drag me back to those rooms
where the demons reside.
I came back from the wasteland
into the bustle of *being*
and birds sing in high places
as I finally arrive.

Simple Thing

I'd like to be an off-beat,
syncopated little thing;
note and stem floating on the melody, just sitting in,
appoggiatura, grace-note, special thing.

I'd like to be a sailor,
swinging on the ocean wind,
coarse old rope between my hands and salt-spray where my toes begin,
nimble little sailor, clever thing.

I'd like to be a bed-sheet,
gentle thing to warm your skin,
thing that you hug tighter when the morning starts to filter in,
falling through your creases, lucky thing.

Steady Now

For most of my life, I think that I've been
in a balancing act on a wobbling beam.
Unstable; a wildcard thrown into the mix,
throwing objects at walls and just seeing what sticks.
And you're solid. I *stay* here. You're tangible and true.
I think that I'll maybe – I might stick to you.

Write Your Daydreams Upon Me

I like you because
you're a kite amongst clouds;
my personal comedy
when skyscrapers chase me
and words blur together
like tragedies.

Tabby

I am a cat on a rooftop.

I sleep in the sun

and watch the wind in the trees

while the world wanders on

like an ocean-bound stream.

I stretch out, lick my feet

and do as I please

like a soft summer morning,

a whimsical dream.

Microcosm

Valentines

get

easier,

my world

gets

simpler,

I become

water

in

sand.

(Even molecules hold hands.)

Sanguinity

One day hope won't be

a storm-cloud's silver lining

but a brilliant sky.

Love

Say It Again

You say "Rose,"
as if I'm something pretty,
a delicate blossom, miniature dance floor full of velvet-skirted
petals and criss-crossing lines,
swirling around and around 'til they're lost in the motion.

You say it tenderly
and like a reminder,
last sound that crackles over the drowning frequency
from leagues away,
calling me back to Earth.

You say it urgently,
as if I was Kate and you were Leo,
ice-bitten flickers of light cast out in that black forsaken ocean
and you wanted me to live.

And the thorns,
do you see them?
Sharp as cutting knives, stiff as greenhouse walls, cold as the winter
outside them,
all to keep away the aphids

So that dancer
foolishly letting the music lead her forward
Won't crumple when it dies.

You say it

surely,

as if by that one syllable

you'd know what I was hiding

and what I was trying, desperately, to find.

Reality is a Stain on the Mirror

And you're still not listening.
But that's one more nasty little detail that I love about you,
like the thick cream in your honey-tea skin,

The way your gold eyes pull me out of the tunnel like headlights
to leave me shivering in the night air
as it chokes all warmth from my body,

And the way you sing me to sleep, draping the melody over me like threads in a cocoon,
Only to have flown in the morning.

And You

Your sword
a shimmer, a trick of the eyes;
a snake dancing this way and that, granting death like
sweet poison,
an art of its own.

Your body
the real weapon
built to last, burning with heat and the heart of a hundred wars
and savagery.
You sing of it; shaking as their cities must
in the white sandstorm
slamming into the bed sheets
while stallions cross the Holy Land.

Your temper
blazing like the blacksmith's forge, steel edge birthed from a fiery
womb,
uncontainable,
unquenchable, aching for the red sun's kiss.

Your eyes
somehow soften.
A blue ocean on a summer's day.
Quiet conversation, on a hillside
miles away.

Coffee Stains

Dress shoes click on the streets laid slick with cinnamon and wasted air.
It's sugar on your lipstick, darling; a dangerous affair.

You chose coffee
like you chose romance
just for the idea of romance; cream and smoked wood swirling
around in your cup,
and steam curling up into the atmosphere like the locks in his hair.

Crushed, bitter,
tantalisingly dark and hauntingly aromatic,
you craved it.
You mocked the raven that eyed you from its branch out in the
blustering courtyard and
you didn't even like the taste.

The silver curve of the teaspoon showed your warped reflection
like a deathly omen.
It showed the line of your neck and each glittering pearl.
The hanging clock on the wall, for all its carved hearts and
varnished oak
couldn't quite drown out the tolling,
ticking,
pendulum swinging by your ear as you ran your hand along the
creases in the leather seat,
The sweet, too-strong perfume mingling with the scent of the

dark black coffee,

concealing,

much as the gold around his wrist had,

the stains in the conversation, the spills on the table and the ice-cold grip of those fevered hands.

Logic Tells Me that Darkness is the Absence of Light

Somehow the black void

behind your bold stare

never seems to come close

to the fall of your hair

and the impact of knowing

the depth of your sin

is removed by the water

running over your skin

and I sift through the pages

but nothing explains

how your burning delusions

got inside of my veins

all the letters and numbers

dissolve into air

as I whisper sweet nothings

to a boy who's not there.

The Closest Thing

Summer days are like crashing waves.
Too fast, too loud, filling my mouth and nose until I can't think
and always a little colder than the memories.

I've never wanted to be swept away.
When each morning is an icy shock, a shove towards the brink,
I want your arms to brace and hold me.

When each glance in the mirror is a tide that I can't swim against
and dreams become sun glares, blinding my eyes.
I'd reach for your lifeboat
to keep me afloat

And dissolve into quietude.
The closest thing to paradise.

Hopelessly

In the yellow creases of bound novels,
eating shadows under the candlelight,
and faraway from frosted windows
where legends dance 'round forest campfires
witnessed by the older-than-magic moon,

In the sway of your robes and the swoop of your messengers,
it's the same old sappy story.
Girl loves everyone
and boy loves girl.

I hate the way
the universe unfolds before you,
fortune climbs towards you
like a puppy, playing to catch that honey gaze.

I hate the peals of daytime laughter that interrupt my midnight
and how you come splashing through the trees,
defying logic as usual,
as if grace when accomplishing the impossible
was something natural.
(And for you, that's probably the case.)

I hate your kindness
at times when I deserve so much less.
Snakelike, I slither and curl,

avert my eyes in self-detest.

I hate the reason in your words,
the clarity,
the way you bring the rest of us back to reality with a smile or an incline of your head.

I strongly dislike
your inconsistent, odd sense of humour.
(I strongly dislike it, and I hate it, too.)

And most of all I hate
that sweet egalitarianism.
Because I want more than anything
to be special to you.

Those Cadences were Crystalline

I recall that you loved her
like you loved jazz,
bright as the gold flecks and swift brass of your movements,
breathing what you sought in the
sine tone of her piano,
grinning as we wowed the crowd
that went up in flames and cheers.

Improvisation was like free-falling,
you weren't sure what you wanted or where you were going
and therein lay the thrill.

I loved you like flute notes and cold breaths on a midwinter
morning,
you loved to hear yourself speak and
I loved how your eyes alit with laughter when you didn't say a
word.
You loved me like a secret smile,
auburn curls and conspiring glances,
loved the distance, maybe,
and the still unmarred proximity.

I pressed you into my memory like manuscripts and printed sheets.
I loved that love was invulnerable, pristine.
I loved the purity of silent glances,

the sweet taste of words unspoken

and the fleeting folly of seventeen.

Love Is an Open-Ended Question

I don't want to fall in love but I do want to love you:
love you like Fridays and three birthday cheers.
Love you like wild schemes and spit on our fingers,
I don't want a romance, I just want you near.

I want to love you like sailboats and daring adventures,
your friends and my friends and long, late night calls.
I want to wander for six months and have my heart broken,
want you to show me it's never quite broken at all.

I want to love you like Plato and pizzas and parties,
sparklers when we're thirty, barefoot and still free.
I want to love you on the sofa when you're dancing and dizzy,
new books and bad movies and you next to me.

Love is for all those who beg to be broken.
It's a story to scare us, make us nod and behave.
When I'm lost in the night without purpose or car keys
I want to land on your doorstep; claim your warmth until day.

I want to love you like jumpers and chalk on the pavement,
poking fun at whatever, baking cakes the wrong way.
I've never seen something to want in sad love songs,
painting colours that only dissolve into grey,

But I'll love you like a restaurant with no reservations,
like that trivia night we guessed all the right things to say.
You cheered and you spun me around, we were laughing,
you said "Get used to winning, 'cause I'm here to stay."

Fancy

I want you softly,
like the cotton against your skin,
like a warm breath on a pale night.

I want you quietly,
like the birds in the steeples,
like the hush before the church bells' ring.

I want you loudly,
like the traffic rush when it gets too much,
like the pains you take to keep me safe,
like a child's delight when the birds take flight.

Let me fall.

I want you roughly without either of us
ever giving in.

Lucidity

Inside my messy mind, you're clear.

Sparse Kindling

Finding your love is like gathering frozen branches.

My hands ache, my teeth chatter.

But I won't last the winter without something for the flames.

We Used to Make Butterfly Hands

You told me that when I was older I would understand
and I looked up and saw the sky in paper planes and periwinkle
blue.
I reached out and drew a line for you;
traced it all over the globe and back to your wise heart
so that when I was older, my head full of understanding,
I'd be able to navigate back to my place there
and touchdown, settle down with you.

You said that our worlds were too distant,
you with your job and bills to pay and me with my honey-sweet
dreams.
I nodded and pulled back my flyaway hair
thinking that if we're alive together, against all the odds and
centuries, alive together,
that's close enough for me.

I kissed you and you told me I was great. Carousel great. Sandy-toes great. Smiles on a Saturday, belly-laughs great.

You snapped the string and flew away.

I'm older now and I do understand
that dotted lines get tangled or just fall away completely and
you were right when you said that things aren't quite as pretty
as they are in my party-hat head.

I'll draw new things for you and cheer on my birthdays for you and hope that one day you find somewhere nice to land.

Flashes

Sometimes when I touch something warm

it's your skin that I feel in the shower again.

I draw my hand away like it's been scalded and flit back

to the present. Safe. The moment's gone.

The past is a vision of bubbly and rings, ski-trips and promises that

sounded so full –

the future is a whirlwind of parties and high spirits,

calendar dates, change and someone else's grin.

But *now*, darling. Now is a lonely thing.

Infinity

I'm afraid that you'll love me like the wind loves daisies,
blowing them over the edge of their precipice overlooking the sea.
I'm afraid you'll meet me sadly at the bottom and lap the water like
a question against my crumpled stem
when the strength of your love has left me numb.
You ask me what I'm afraid of, and I'm afraid that you're a nebula
spanning the vast darkness of space
while I'm just a lonely speck of sand;
too small not to get swept up in your currents and dragged out into
the rolling ocean
and lose myself forever beneath your stars.

Things I'd like to Tell You – A Shortlist

v. If I knew of a way to fuse our brain synapses together and show you that I love you, well – I probably wouldn't do it. Because that's creepy. And also I don't have a medical degree. So until I get a medical degree and potentially break a few laws in the name of passion or science, you'll just have to take my word for it. I love you. I love you. If love is a thing caused by rushes of dopamine, I'm probably suffering from dopamine toxicity. The doctors should probably check me for that.

iv. I want you to know about my band posters. Isn't that weird? I want you to know that I can be crazy about things, and that sometimes I close my eyes and I'm a ten-year-old who wants to be a horse-whisperer again. Mostly I want you to know that I'm crazy about you.

iii. I want to know things about *you* – like, I want to know if you prefer winter or summer. And I want to groan-but-not-actually-judge-you when you say winter, because everybody fucking says winter, don't they? I don't know how they can stand it. Winter, that is. I'm always freezing. Even in summer, I'm freezing all the time.

ii. I like getting warmer with you.

i. I make a lot of lists. But I've never attempted to make a list of things about you, because it would probably be impossible, you know? You're one of those infinite things. Like the sky, or juice flavours, or songs that I like from the nineties. Most things sort of come to a stop for me, but you just go on and on.

Lover

If you wish to hold my heart, don't encase it.

Hold it like the string of a kite.

Lift it up into the serene blue and watch it fly.

Unexpected Goodbye

I am a mess, as raw and undefined
as rough streaks of paint suggesting birds in the sky
and I'm sorry to give you my wild-hued whirls;
you, who deserves the luminous world.

Blank Prescription

In the town that I loved
by the beach that I loved
on the cast-away street that I loved, that I loved,
I strayed into the cinema to see the stars that I loved.

They twisted my head and caught hold of my hair,
sighed softly and murmured, *no, little dear.*
This.
This is how you love.

Then they showed me their scenes
until the scenes laced my dreams
and I was left chasing echoes of love.

I walked out into daylight and ever since then
the doubt
the doubt
the doubt has set in
a little more each time that I've laughed, cried, made a friend -
Is it real? Enough? Is it love?

I want to chase them and scream
that I *care for this world*
from each lungful of air to each shivering cloud
and my love isn't theirs to box in or shut out

and they're wrong

but I love, love, love, love them.

Summer Love

People speak of

summer love

like it's worth more than love in winter,

like it crunches beneath fall branches

and escapes spring's fleeting hold.

They revere it

like it lasts longer

than the time it takes for summer

to appear, flash once and filter

out; like summer stays so long.

Infinite Truths

If it is true

that there are places in the galaxy

where time is not linear

and existence is cyclic,

that every moment can exist all at once,

reality fractured into countless seconds

and that the people we love never leave us

then it must also be true

that in some small way,

somewhere,

you still belong to me.

Message in a Bottle

That night your lips pressed down like a sealed envelope
and all the ways I could think of to say 'I'm sorry' didn't seem to
cut it
so I stayed silent in the deafening storm
and watched you drift further away.

Now across the table you're a distant shore
but I don't want to be your message in a bottle.
I want us together
right here.

Late-Night Conversations

We talk until it's late.
You say, "I'd better let you go,"
but you never do, you know.
I fall asleep and wish I was awake.

At the End of the Day

You come home late
skirting my questions like landmines
as if with one wrong move I'd detonate.
I switch off the TV, come to bed and stay awake.
I watch you sleep and
it's just not the same.

Daffodil

Braver than battalions, brighter than balloons,
we used to be summer's heralds months before it came.
We danced like maybe everything was only effervescence
and you told me I was every pop-song mixing into one.

You invite me to a party but I don't want them to see
that we don't dance the way we used to,

we don't sing the words the same.

These days music speaks to me of all the things I'd rather be.
These days, you hesitate before you say my name.

Saturday

You draw smiling faces on train windows
because even city transport can't get away unaffected
by your cheer.
I like you, I like you, I like you
when you're tired like moth-wings and fresh like spring mornings
and even my worst days are lovely
when you're near.

Sovereigns

Cold crown, haunting melody,
wake me up before you leave,
you have battlefields to meet,
I have your face to see.

Lines adorn my once-smooth hands,
lines from managing affairs
of state and coin and our people's cares
so I comb them through your hair.

You smile, they see their wild hero,
I see a soul too tired to know
what'll happen in that field of snow
but I know you're coming home.

So now, two burdened hearts, we stand,
you're still my teenage new best friend
held close for this one moment
in our hope, our love, our land.

Handheld

Cool hands on summer skin,

face the tide and pull me in.

I'd walk barefoot on nebula stars,

you'd fly to me and heal the scars.

We'd take off into velvet night,

they'd navigate by our love's bright light.

There's no such thing as far away

when your heart is my place to stay.

Love

Love isn't an object.
It can't be defined.
It is beauty immeasurable;
destinies entwined.

And scholars could school it
and scientists scope it,
but ever elusive
is that flight unconfined.

People

Red Riding Hood

I want to believe people so badly when they say they won't bite
that I contemplate climbing into their smiling jaws,
thinking that it might be better to be split in two than left hanging.
But always, I draw my red hood and flit back into the forest,
running in the shadows of pathways, never stepping into clearings,
because I've spent my whole life in the wilderness
and I still can't tell the wolves from the woodsmen.

Small Town

I was born in a town between

sleep and insomnia

and they taught me to walk quietly

so I wouldn't wake the dead.

I nod along and watch my step

but I don't have the heart to tell them

that the dead dance on hillsides when the moonlight is cold

and it's the living I'm truly afraid of.

The Secret Keeper

Meet me at the water's edge
where the day's last sunlight hits the waves
in sharp, thin lines of silver-white
that only we will see.

Meet me when the townsfolk hush
and candlelight flickers through window-glass,
for these grey hours are my glistening gold
beyond dreams of kings and queens.

Meet me in shadows and meet me in faith.
Meet me in valleys between summer hills.
Bring me your secrets, such measureless riches.
Bring me your secrets. I'll keep them.

Rapunzel

Each visit to the outside world is a fifty-foot drop
from a lonely tower
shattering and reforming my mind in an instant.
Voices call to the blinded prince and the girl out searching
for a god who doesn't take the shape of her mother
but she sees roads and cities and monstrous things.
There's a memory of purity:
a warm bed and a single window,
the light an open, welcoming blue.
But is the memory mine?
Or did I simply claim it?
Oh, Rapunzel, Rapunzel,
I don't know who I am.
I think that if I go back to the clouds and the birdsongs,
maybe my heart will be cleansed.

Greetings from the Glimmering Grove

We fly because we always look up

to the undersides of toadstools like thatched roofs and warm ovens;

to the moss of forest tree trunks (there's no colour more ancient than green);

to the swan-wings and firefly lights

like changing constellations

and to the sun who loved us and loves us still.

We fly because the air lines our wings

and keeps us aloft, just as simply as spider-webs sing

with the dew-drops each morning,

it's natural to love them,

like the sun who loved us and loves us still.

Conversation Piece

This dress is a conversation piece.
Unclasp it, talk me out of it; take the words away from me.
We learn the rules to break them; we build cages to walk free –
what does my lipstick colour matter now, when red is all you see?

The Wanderer

She decided that trusting in others
was like trying to scrub the mildew out of alleyways – useless.
Amidst the damp darkness, the grit and doubt would always grow back.
So she packed her bag and laced her shoes,
counted her pennies and left the threadbare city
to find somewhere she could rest her head without drowning her heart.
She dreamed of rolling fields and found a bicycle with broken wheels.
She rode until it fell apart, and dreamed of rolling fields.
She dreamed of clear blue skies and found an aeroplane with creaking wings.
She held on tight and landed somewhere blanketed in snow.
She wandered on and trusted in
the crooked road, her newfound home,
to take her somewhere growing green with love and rich with hope.

Communication

I'd plug a microphone into my mind
if that would help me speak it.
The message is always incomplete
by the time it gets to you.

I want to believe that communication is more
than tapping the pane of a TV screen
and twisting bad antennae
hoping something filters through.

I have tried and I have tried
to believe that we can synchronise
but I'm never on your network
and you're never watching mine.

There must be something more than what we know,
some higher frequency.
Because words have made me feel powerful so many times
and so many times they have failed me.

Expiration

With you I always feel like I'm
trying
   to break in the wrong size of shoes.
Sometimes I sit and stew
over how you're seventeen and
you think I'm a princess,
  the trapped-in-a-tower kind,
      and how you wear suits and talk about politics
and think you know the world.

My throat interrupts with a gurgling sound
sometimes when I think about you,

 and how
you deal out advice where it just isn't called for
you quote science-fiction to justify war
and you're seventeen years old and you think I'm a princess
and you just have no blooming idea.

Darling, one of these days I will tell you my mind
But until then we'll never fit
                    right.

In truth
I'm afraid –
that even after that day,

you'll still be trimmed hedges and high picket fences
when I want a field, open wide.

Last Night (Speeding Onwards)

The stars screamed last night, and your hair
your hair was ablaze in the last shreds of sun,
extinguished by the globe's reckless spin as I accelerated harder,
the gears never faltering,
summer down here is approaching so fast.
I don't care for costumes but when you discard them
my heart tears out a rhythm to put tom-toms to shame
you pulled your hair back over your kerosene shoulder
and tore off whatever thing caught your interest this year.
I think I forgot what it means to *October*,
I don't think that's even a verb, I don't care
summer down here is approaching like cyclones
bad things and good things obscured by your gaze and
I want you to scare me,
say you love me and scare me,
cut the breaks from the engine and honestly scare me,
your candour is like summer; inescapable, ruthless,
last night the stars were all shouting your name.

Hotline

The kettle was boiling the first time I called you. It was strange to hear that sound;
a cold house stirring out of hibernation with the tiniest of actions, small activities taking hold.

I didn't think the phone would work. Or that my hands would know the number. I didn't think you'd answer, but you did.

You spoke to me about large things
responsibility and Ferris wheels and distant nebulas
you spoke to me about small things
garden mice and sub-atomic particles and how many spoonfuls of sugar you take with your tea.

I spoke to you about things sometimes
calories and the side-effects of capitalist ideologies
sharpeners with the screws lying on the table and the blades nowhere to be found
about people with so much to say that they talk in their sleep
and how I was never one of them.

Each time that I called you we spoke about new things
I was surprised at the number of conversation topics people can find in a day
I spoke to you about picking mulberries and I laughed when you told me you'd never tasted one.

You spoke to me about thermal currents
about how birds seek them out and they expend a lot of energy at first
but then they find that bubble of warm air and then they're just gliding
And once they've found it the flight becomes simple. Their biology slips into its place.

You told me that there's no such thing as silence. That everything is noisy if you listen closely enough.

I called you less and less often
I was listening to big things like hot fronts and cold fronts
I was noticing all sorts of things, like new jobs and new places to live and how there are cities in Europe where they share all their bicycles,
isn't that nice?

I heard once that all people are made out of star matter
I'm calling now to tell you that I think that it's the other way around:
I think my favourite parts of space are the signals in telephones cables
and how things can change as radically as winter turns to summer.
Last night I traced our conversations back to constellations forming in your voice

and I remember thinking that

the stars are lucky to be made of us.

Plasma

I had a friend tell me that war is the blood between our bones,
That it keeps us moving and
Without it we are stagnant. Nothing.

But I can't see the light in night-drenched dreams.
And I'm sure that cannot be.

Peace is a cool kiss on fevered skin,
The silence when the false thunderclaps end,
The skylights holding a promise that morning will come.

Death is not pigments or science or molten gold,
The pillars of civilisation or the illumining crown.

It is blood on a child's skin. Words that will never come home.
Mothers that will never find air to breathe again.

Peace is a sight unknown to my mind,
But it's the only beauty worth believing in.

Pavement Picasso

Hopscotch,
minute watch,
an hour of Simon Says.

You're the only one who knows me,
you're the only one who cares.

Guess-my-name,
soccer game,
dirty little rhyme.

Let's run away and waste a day
going back in time.

Absence

I still hear your voice in the wide open meadow,
laughing like honey bees
and Currawong cries.
In the shivering of gum leaves
and the shadows of steam trains,
spied between fences and snowflakes' tears.
I still hear your voice at the foot of the staircase
by the swing-set at sunrise,
in the car when it rains.
In the whisper of piano keys that play every evening
and haven't been touched in years.

Lorelei

Tonight I heard a mermaid sigh.
Though she lay where sailors fear to go,
I found her cove and met her eyes,
and asked her why she fretted so.

Her hand reached out and clasped my hair.
She smiled at me with icy breath,
She told me there was beauty there
and bade me to join her in the ocean depths.

I held still and considered this.
Her nails were sharp against my skin,
but her song was sweet and the sea was calm.
I acquiesced and let her draw me in.

Her scales glinted and her eyes were keen,
she grinned and pulled me underneath.
We left the cove unheard, unseen,
unobstructed by man or boat or reef.

I sensed in her a manic drive,
in her grip, her laugh, her steely edge,
and the ocean now seemed great, alive,
waiting, roaring for my pledge.

She offered me a pearl so bright,
so pure, so whole, so round and smooth
that its shimmering warded off the night
and revealed to me a thousand truths.

And now I've heard the canon sweet
and now I've known the mermaid's cry
I'll never want for soil or feet,
or to feel the woes of the starved and dry.

No earthly quarrels can weigh my brow,
where sea-salt scents the open air,
where the ocean is my eternal tower
where the dulcet tones light my mermaid's hair.

Supernova

It was a '67 orange Chevrolet,
tinted windows, spattered paint
and the smell of hot sauce that never quite left.
Leather kept the warmth of better summers,
dancing shoes and faded denim
gas like heaven on these city streets.

And wherever they went they took fireworks with them,
bursts of colour in the blackened sky,
Just like popping paint balls against the drop sheets,
making love when there were backs to break and wars to see,
no different than
sunset orange,
a chugging engine, sand and burning feet.

Years later it still ran smooth like memories
of slapping wasps and tipsy victories,
giving freely of their speckled innocence
and gaining something bittersweet.

The Straw House

Little pig, little pig,
let me come in.
Do you remember when fancies were shiny and new?
There wasn't a hair on your chinny-chin-chin,
and our toes chilled on floorboards before we dipped them in.
Our mothers held us tightly and our troubles were few.

Little pig, little pig,
please tell me the time?
Am I too rough and ragged, a gruff wolverine?
You once talked for hours, sharing tales and rhymes,
eyes alight with the spilling of secrets sublime
and now I'm too sickly and grey to be seen.

Little pig, little pig,
just spare me a glance,
or a word or a smile or a sentence or two.
I don't ask for blessings, I don't want to dance
or to sing or weave stories of adventure and romance.
All I ask before we part
if you have the good heart,
is for a sweet recollection of when our troubles were few.

Identity

Hypotheticals

I could talk about myself forever, you know.

I could lean across the lounge, lay my head on your shoulder and just breathe myself into your skin

and maybe you'd be too drunk to hear the mumbling.

I wouldn't care. I'd make believe that you were listening.

I'm not a liar

but I don't know if I'm honest, either.

People say *twenty-something* like it's supposed to carry meaning

and I've never, I never, I'll never fit in.

When I was six I tricked my classmates into thinking I had a real nose ring.

I danced without care. I won a prize just for smiling.

I wish I was still that girl

instead of a bundle of hair and ribs and wonky thoughts,

vainly trying to straighten out,

always stumbling into things.

I could listen to you forever, though.

I'd sink like a stain into the cushions and

make believe that I was talking.

I'm good at that kind of thing.

Admission

I want to

tell you

that

I was never

much of a

liar

and

when it comes

to

fight or flight

I spread

my wings

and fly.

That humour is

my

survival instinct

and

I hate

a world

where kindness is

a poison

to be sucked dry.

But I can tell you also

that

when birds make nests

I let them be

and that

I'll catch your smile when it falls

so you'll never lose it

and that

when harsh words and city streets

get too much for me

I hold my ears

sing *'la, la, la,'*

and I'll lose no sleep

over feeling free

or choosing latter

over

former

in the word

bittersweet.

Survival is a Balancing Act

I want to be hard,
a sceptic cased in iron and stone; voice like winter rain
to tell the world that it may never hurt me.

But I want to be soft,
soft like the first peach of the season, honest like my parents taught me,
sunny as the day I was born.

Huntress

You are not delicate.

You are an Amazon warrior stringing her bow. You are made of the same rains that fall hard with her footfalls
while war-songs tear through the night and the whole forest vibrates.

You are mighty. Nothing breaks you. You are wildfire dancing on stone.

Red Stains on Winter Graves

In another life

I was not a rose but a soldier.

I died a hundred times

far from home

on fallen snow.

You take my arm and twirl me 'round

But I've seen things you'll never know.

You can kiss the knife

between my teeth

but you'll never be my hero.

The Wall of Sound

My mind is a coconut radio –
a small spark of human life
on an uncharted island,
sending *short – long – short, short – long – short,*
crying to connect to the planes overhead.

My personality is a collection of half-developed photographs,
someone else always the artist
and I, the film left overnight in the darkened studio,
ideas that might never see daylight
or might dazzle the world from a gallery wall.

My life up to this point has been the screech of brakes before the crash
and I, the unaware, sleeping passenger.
We break the wall of sound
and in the aftermath, as sirens call,
I see the shattered car window, its own life-force bleeding.
I watch my reflection, staggering now.
I don't want my voice to drown out.

Navigating Labyrinths

You tell me that I'm delicate and I don't bother disagreeing.
Not out loud, anyway.
I'm too accustomed to softening the edges of my opinions
or not stating them at all, and

sometimes I'm stronger than a siren's call. A waterfall.
But sometimes I'm twenty-one and still a bully's easy target
and the pressure of explaining myself just gets too much to bear.

People say *'don't let others define you'* and it's like holding back armadas;
stopping a fleet from hitting the shore
and I'm sick of other people being right about me
without trying to dig deeper at all.

I'm a fire nymph; I want to burn whole worlds to their foundations.
I want to tear up my poetry;
communicate in a way that matters
because every effort seems ineffectual and I don't want to be left voiceless.

When predators cast their gazes at me, I want them to turn into stone.

It Seems Like Everybody Writes About Romance

When I was six a girl with golden hair told me that *'true love's first kiss'* would break all spells
as if for every single problem I would need somebody else
and there are things that I'm too scared to say
through poetry most days –

like how last night I Googled aromantic
and how I'm sick of feeling disconnected
and how I lie through my teeth in my writing sometimes
just to feel like I'm doing alright.

But lately I've stopped giving a damn
what they say about love, because I –
I love in ways that they cannot define.
Love is raw. It's unstructured. I'm fine.

Green

I think I was one of the green children. Buried in me is a garden.
I think I'm growing from the outside in.
Visitors reach out to touch me, and
my blossoms are wilting
branches drooping from the weight of all the things that I can't take.
I close the gate against their onslaughts, but they still come in.

When the Lights Go Down and it's You in the Ring

Optimism is not a sweetened cake.
Optimism is a decision you make
when your mind's been on fire for five years straight
and sometimes you have to make it thirty-eight times a day
again and again and again.

When you were six your dad told you this:
you have to learn to fall the right way
and roll over, keep your wits sharp, get up again;
keep your belly guarded just the same.

So I fight and fight back for survival's sake.
This is the decision I make.
This is the decision I make.
This is the decision I make again.

Art

Here's What Doesn't Hurt

It's about the words:

the comfortable rhythm of fingers on keypads

like heat and sound making your body sway to an even tempo,

the future forgotten, the present forgotten,

the past forgotten.

It's about the songs:

not the legacy or the people in the crowd,

but the homage to a simple sound.

I want it to feel as natural as dancing.

Ambition is a trap and so is complacency,

it hurts to *want* and it hurts to *be*

but here's what doesn't hurt:

the flow, the rhythm, the words.

Paint until There's Only Positive Space

I am the street artist; rough clothes and thin visage.
You are the city, vivacious and loud.
Night after night, I find myself in dark places
spraying colours on your faces just to talk to you.

Have you ever tagged a train?
The art I envy is like you –
making waves at night to leave the landscape brighter in the day.
You are the cause I just want to connect with:
fresh, something different, something new.

Gossamer

Poetry has gossamer wings
and she flies and she flies and she flies.
She spins her nest out of fragments and whims
and parades it through midsummer skies.

And those who would catch her come stealthily,
those who'd hold her would hold their own eyes,
and those who would know her would gaze at the clouds
where she flies and she flies and she flies.

Performer

She never felt safer than up on the stage

with a heart like a sparrow released from a cage

to trust in the words and the golden bright lights,

to trust in the art like a leap from great heights.

And she learned to trust, not because of the plays

but because of the warmth of her playfellow's gaze

and she built herself castles to last for an age

With the strength that she gathered from up on the stage.

Truth in the Lens

Your 35mm camera
is like a kid's scrawl on a cement wall: *we were here.*
Passion unabridged,
documentation for the sake of documentation
as we lose track of what we were supposed to be doing
and just exist.
You're as raw as a light scratch at three in the morning,
as lost as a Polaroid in that pocket in your suitcase
that you always forget is there.
(You're not really lost at all.)

www.ingramcontent.com/pod-product-compliance
Lightning Source LLC
Chambersburg PA
CBHW031424290426
44110CB00011B/515